Paradise Loot

by Don Blanding

Petroglyph Press, Ltd.

Illustrations by
DON BLANDING
JULIETTE JESSIE MAE FRASER
A. S. MACLEOD
JOHN KELLY
Illustrations for "Baby Street" and "Jasmine House" by
IWILANI BASLER

PUBLISHED BY THE PETROGLYPH PRESS, LTD.
160 KAMEHAMEHA AVENUE • HILO, HAWAI'I 96720
808-935-6006 / FAX 808-935-1553
reedbook@interpac.net
www.basicallybooks.com

ISBN 0-912180-55-2

FIRST EDITION ~ 1924
FIRST PRINTING BY THE PETROGLYPH PRESS ~ 1979

SECOND PETROGLYPH PRESS EDITION
NEW TYPESETTING AND ADDITIONAL ILLUSTRATIONS
Copyright 2000
FIRST PRINTING ~ MAY 2000

Contents

*I give you as greeting from Hawaii all of the
sunshine that the silk-petalled cup of an
hibiscus blossom can hold.*

To those of you who made this dreamer's
        dream come true . . . .
gave me my year of great adventure. . . let me
        dream anew . . .
most gratefully I dedicate my book to you.

WORTHLESS treasures and priceless
    trash,
Silver that gleams in the lightning's flash,
Gold that the sunset spills on the sky,
Gauzes and tissues in mists trailing by,
Diamonds, a necklace of dew on the grass,
Filagree silver in frost on the glass,
Lace in kiawe-trees shadowing brooks,
Riches a money-blind man overlooks,
Perfumes of Araby scenting a lane,
Opals that fall from the sky in the rain,
Gold in the sands of a shallow lagoon;
Platinum dripping cold white from the moon,
Silk in the rose petals flung on the breeze,
Velvet in moss on the trunks of the trees,
Day-dreams and memories, moments acute
With thrice-distilled happiness—vagabond's
        loot.

DREAMER

I DON'T suppose I'll ever see
   A dryad slipping from her tree
Nor hear the pulsing pipes of Pan
(altho, at times, I think I can)
Nor see the moon-nymphs dance at night
And yet, perhaps–perhaps I might.

I watch the waves break on the rocks
And in between the thundered shocks
I think that I can almost hear
The sirens singing sweet and clear.

Sometimes the shadows on a tree
Like dappled fauns appear to me
And once beside a blue lagoon
Beneath a witching tropic moon
I saw the flash of silver scales
(The kind that grow on mermaid's tails).

I don't suppose I'll ever see
These things that mean so much to me
But if I watch by night, by day,
You can not tell–perhaps I may.

LUAU

CAN'T you feel the happy tingle . . .
    Can't you hear the snappy jingle
    Of the jazzy ukulele . . . it's a cheerful
      sound and pert?
Can't you hear the deeper throbbing
And the sentimental sobbing
    Of the steel guitars a-crying like a laugh
      that hides a hurt?

On the table, leis of maile
Sweetly fragrant peeping shyly
    From the blazing red hibiscus and the moun-
      tain-green of ti.
How your appetite does quicken
When you see the bowls of chicken
    And the poi—oh boy—why some folks
      never like it puzzles me.

See the salty mounds of limu
And the pig hot from the imu;
    See the smoking sweet potatoes and the
      mullet wrapped in leaves.
Little nips of roast kukui,
Squid and luau, rich and gooey—
    That's the thing you praise to folks away
      and nobody believes.

Fresh opihis there to munch on;
Little crabs to crack and crunch on;
    Shrimp and lobster, luscious wana . . . .
      What comes last and what comes first?
Use your fingers—don't be fussy
Though it is a trifle mussy;
    You'll enjoy it and you'll gorge yourself
      until you nearly burst.

Here's a cup–don't ask what's in it.
Drink it down–in just a minute
    You'll be gayer than the gayest with your
       troubles left behind.
See those smiling kindly faces.
Well, I've been a lot of places
    But I've never found a welcome like the
       Honolulu kind.

There's the moon just faintly showing
Through the torches' orange glowing.
    Someone sing a song–an old song–not this
       modern whah-whah jazz.
"Imi au"–that song of longing
Sets old memories to thronging
    There's a poignancy about it that no other
       love song has.

Getting late–a few are yawning.
In the sky a hint of dawning.
    Gone the fish and pig and luau–gone the
       bowls of creamy poi.
Don't you hate to hear them starting
That one perfect song of parting
like a plucking on your heart-strings "'Til
we meet . . . aloha oe."

JASMINE HOUSE
In Honolulu

The flagstone walk to Jasmine House
    Is full of lazy casual curves;
      To right it leads, to left it swerves
Then to the door. Would you arouse
          The folks within?
          Then make a din,
          They'll let you in.

Above the door the jasmine grows
    Abloom with stars . . . each star as white
    As any in the sky at night
And twice as many . . . goodness knows !
          With lots and lots
          Of ferns in pots
          In shady spots.

The monkey pods spread out above
 The little house to keep it cool,
 And hyacinths float in a pool
Where mynahs bathe. The flowers love
   To blossom there
   Where people care
   How flowers fare.

The roof is red. From peak to eaves
 The morning glories make display
 With moons of pink and blue asway.
Below the ginger blooms in sheaves.
   A lovely show
   Like perfumed snow
   These flowers blow.

Banana trees wave tattered flags.
 Begonias shed their petal tears,
 Around the corner boldly peers
A bougainvillea clad in rags.
   Such rags you've seen
   A gypsy queen
   Wear . . . red and green.

This house that bears the jasmine name
 Is just the sort I'd like to own,
 From ruddy roof to walk of stone
With flowers wild and flowers tame.
   A tropic bit.
   It seems to fit.
   I'm fond of it.

THE CANDLE MAKER

A cubby-hole, dark dingy gray
    Tucked in between two little stores
    With stagnant tubs of fish about
      And bowls of Chinese sauerkraut
      And vegetables strewn on the floors
The candle-maker sits all day.

He looks as old as time itself
    His face is but a wrinkled mask,
      Thin body, like a gargoyle, bent
      Above his pools of paint, content.
To dream in paint and wax, his task.
The dreams, as candles, line a shelf.

With tallow fat on bamboo wicks,
  With patterns from a 'broidered shawl.
    With careful brush and Chinese skill
    He works his wizardry until
  Strange flowers bloom and dragons crawl
Along fantastic candle-sticks.

A sudden thick vermillion splash,
  A subtle green that has no name
    A wavered line of antique gold,
    Cerise, celestial blue—behold!
  A phoenix rising from the flame
Where seven colors shriek and clash.

"Good luck, long life" is written there
  Upon each stick in letters bold,
    So in your painted candle's glow
    Wherever you may be, you'll know
  The curling blue-gray smoke will hold
For you a kindly Chinese prayer.

And with the smoke your thoughts will stray
  To where, between two little stores
    With stagnant tubs of fish about
    And bowls of Chinese sauerkraut
  And vegetables strewn on the floors,
The candle-maker paints all day.

SONS OF THE SURF

Gods of the sea . . . like winging gulls
    they soar,
Light as the spray that stings their bronzy
      breasts,
    Swift as the wind that races them to shore,
Sons of the surf that bears them on its crests.

BLACK POINT

Line after line the green battalions of the sea
  Charge to defeat against the fortress of the
    land;
  Charge and retreat in white surrender to the
    sand;
Troops of a war in which no armistice can be.

Year after year the waves with wild unceasing
    roar
  Bludgeon and beat the silent, black, defend-
    ing rocks
  Counting as victory ten thousand thundered
    shocks
To gain one grain of sand torn from the shore.

ALMOST ANY NIGHT

Moonlight gilding silver sword blades of the
   palms
   That clash soft music in the breeze above
   my door;
   Moonlight spilling silver coins upon my floor
And filling flower cups with wine that sweetly
   calms.

Moonlight weaving gauzy veils of crystal white
   Afloat on tangled webs of haunting melody,
   Tracing a gleaming path across a dreaming
   sea,
Working white magic through a long Hawaiian
   night.

Bon Voyage

When you decide to go away
    You must not say that we are cold
Or scold because we act so gay
    And laugh and chaff and do not hold
You to our heart or weep or cry
    Or say good-bye. You see, we know
Before you go that you will try
    To stay away a year or so
But ere the year has gone, we're sure
    That you will wish with might and main
That you were here. You'll feel the lure
    And come galumphing back again.

At the Ruins of an Ancient Heiau

YOU are an unlovely lot,
    You scatterers of paper bags and cracker
       boxes,
Clumping with loud, stupid feet
Where bronze, majestic gods have walked.
    Have you no reverence?

This great black altar,
Lava rock and coral,
Staring bleakly to the sky
Has known the prayers and songs of worship-
      pers,
Vibrated to drums,
Echoed the strong voice of chants
And caught the whisper of old invocations.
These were the gods of a great people,
Born of an historic past,
Glorified by legend,
And clothed with the dreams of forgotten poets.
Dying to make place for other gods.

    The need of gods is old–and ever new.

You who can not sense the beauty in the
      dreams of other races,
Whether they be the flame-crowned deities of
      pagans,
The calm-eyed Buddha of the Orient
Or the mud gods of the black Africans
Can not know and value
Our own pale suffering Christ.

Shadows of the Gods

DRIFTERS

Some of us drift to these shores on the trade-
    winds;
    Drift here and linger. The days slip along
Autumn and summer, the spring and the winter
    Pass like the uncounted notes of a song.

Some of our hearts find their roots here and
    blossom.
    Harder each day to depart if one lingers
Hours and days and the months and the seasons
    Trickle like water and sand through our
    fingers.

FROM A JAVANESE BATIK IN A FORT
STREET WINDOW

Somewhere white peacocks dream on pedestals
    of twisted brass
    Or spread their pale fantastic fans beneath
    the perfumed ylang-ylang.
Somewhere slim maidens in their gilded gar-
    ments pass
    Strumming the yalvi . . . chanting to its
    slow barbaric twang.

WHEN IT RAINS

TONIGHT the streets are wet with rain.
The moon attempts to shine, in vain.
A kona blows. The palms are torn.
The flowers whipped to rags forlorn
And leaves are strewn along the street
Beneath the hurried, homeward feet
Of people who attempt to find
A shelter. No one seems to mind
So very much. They simply wait
Until the wind and rain abate,
Then go about their own affairs.
It rains so gaily, no one cares.

MOVIES IN HONOLULU

Gray shadows on a silver sheet
   Triumphant beauties . . . aged hags,
   In royal robes . . in beggar's rags
When vice and virtue nightly meet.

A princess in her castle swoons;
   A vampire shows her snaky curves;
   A villain gets what he deserves;
A mother to her baby croons.

The Movie News, in pictures, shows
   The native dance of Samarkand,
   The beauties of Somaliland,
Or how a striped orchid grows;

All shadow-play . . . all mummer's parts,
   A story on a whirling reel
   And yet a thousand people feel
These mimic passions stir their hearts.

And thus a little Chinese miss
   May be du Barry for an hour
   Or Sleeping Beauty in her bower
Awaiting that enchanted kiss.

Thus Tiki San or Mary Green
   Or Ferdinand or you or I,
   May live and love and do and die
Synthetically upon the screen.

For seven nations mix and meet
   In absolute democracy
   Sans sham and sans hypocrisy
Where shadows cross the silver-sheet.

BABY STREET
(Down Palama Way)

I walk quite slowly down Baby Street
Babies are everywhere . . . under my feet,
Sprawled on the sidewalks, perched on the
    walls,
Babies in dydies, in blue overalls,
Babies in rompers of flowered cretonne,
Babies with not much of anything on,
Little brown babies in brown mamas' laps.
Philippine babies, Koreans and Japs,
Fresh, shiney babies right out of the tub,
Babies in scandalous need of a scrub,
Baby Hawaiians, the sons of a chief,
Rastus from Africa, black past belief,
Babies with yellow hair, babies with brown,
Babies with just a few patches of down,
Toddling babies on little bowed legs,
Very new babies much balder than
    eggs,
Portuguese babies, and Russians as well,
Babies whose ancestors no one can tell,
Toothless as turkeys . . . these tiny young tads,
But grinning as though they were dentifrice ads.

Walk very carefully . . . make your step hesitant.
One of these babies may some day be president.

23

KOA TREES

The times ten thousand crescent moons
  Are pendant in the koa trees
Green-gold beneath the sun of noons,
  Green-silver in the evening breeze.

BROCADE

WHAT is the pattern and fabric of our
      love?
Moonlight, drawn through silver mists
By the witchery of night-winds on Tantalus.
    Darkly velvet, the shadows of koa leaves
Fall in curved delicacy, shifting and touching
Like lips that lightly touch and touch again.
    Raindrops pierce the dimly shadowed lines
Like crystal beads, tossed across an old and
        lovely tapestry.
    In swift flowing line, clean, glinting,
Runs the red-gold thread of ecstasy
And by it the twilight mauve of sadness
Giving the rich gold a brighter gleam.
    Here and there, in no arranged design,
Are rare, fine jewels . . . .
Fire-opals, burning with a lambent flame
Amethysts, deeply purple as a sorrow,
Lapis, bluely restful,
And one deep sapphire
Holding in its heart a white radiance
Like that first star we saw at evening . . .
    These are our little moments of happiness.

Koa Trees

AT ST. CLEMENTS ON WILDER AVENUE

A SHADY residential street,
    A little church sedate and neat
With sun-browned walls and slanted roof,
Quite dignified . . . a bit aloof
From all the clamor of the day
Yet friendly in its quiet way.

I wandered by. To my surprise . . .
Could I believe my startled eyes . . .
Someone had flung a Spanish shawl
Above the door, against the wall
With vivid green . . . a scarlet splash
And orange like a cymbal's crash.
A gaily pagan bold expanse
Of gorgeous color dissonance.

Of course it was no Spanish shawl
That blazed against that quiet wall.
A sweetheart vine had climbed and hung
Its orange blossoms all among
A bougainvillea's purple blooms.

I hope no prudish soul presumes
To touch that joyous color scheme
Because those happy flowers seem
To try in their sweet silent way
To sing a hymn of praise, I'd say.

TORCH-LIGHT FISHERMEN

Flaring lines of orange lights
　　Like fire-flies appear to me
　　Above the reef off Waikiki.
They glow and dim. The sight delights.

So gay they are against the night!
　　I know they're simply men who fish
　　With torches. Just the same, I wish
That they *were* fire-flies in flight.

DIAMOND HEAD

The empty setting for some great jewel of
the sun torn from its resting place centuries
before time began.

KILAUEA

Patterns of fury etched in flame.

SECRET PLACE

There's a place in Manoa—way up in the
    hills—
    Where the forest comes down like an army
    in green;
Where the gossamer sheen of a waterfall spills
      And is flung by the breeze
      To the rocks and the trees
And the thrushes—shy singers—are heard
    and not seen.

It is there that the ginger blows, fragrant and
    white;
    Where climbing lianas trail down from the
    sky;
And the ferns make a canopy, lacy and light;
      There's a spring that is cool
      Flowing into a pool
And a gay little brook that goes burbling by.

The shadows that fall from the leaves to the
    grass
    Are rags of black velvet on emerald plush
And the clouds dim the sunlight to gray as
    they pass
      Where the day filters through
      To the slender bamboo
    And a sly, slinky mongoose slips out of the
    brush.

If I look through the curtains of leaves hanging
     down
   I can see tiny glimmers of dazzling blue
With patches of turquoise and blotches of
     brown
          With spatters of yellow
          And orange and mellow—
The sea and the sky and the roofs of the town.

It's quiet and peaceful and restful and cool;
     It's secret—it's mine—this lost little spot;
I go there to think and to dream by the pool
          All alone, quite, unless—
          I don't blush to confess—
That's it's nicer with someone I love a whole
     lot.

29

CURRY

LOBSTER curry on mounds of rice.
 If you like curry it's mighty nice
With grated coconut, feathered down,
Little green onions frizzled brown,
Nuts and the yolks of hard-boiled eggs,
Mango chutney and garlic pegs,
Anchovy paste and Bombay duck,
Bits of bacon and Hindu truck,
Minced green peppers and chow-chow, too,
And anything else that occurs to you.

Mix together . . . a heaping plate.
A dish for a blinking potentate.

QUERY

Why does a little flower, blue and gay, go
By such a gastly name as this . . plumbago?

A RESPONSE

I WROTE of my house of dreams one day
My 'Vagabond's house.' I told the way
That the rugs were laid across the floor
I told of the walls and the panelled door,
I told of the books on a teak-wood stand,
The bits of lacquer, the Concert-Grand,
The favorite pictures on the wall
The woven silk of a faded shawl,
The jars of spices along a shelf,
I told of the things I chose myself
To grace my house . . . those priceless things
That an hour of idle dreaming brings.

So vividly real it sometimes seemed
That I quite forgot that I only dreamed;
That the walls were smoke, that the colors gay
Were a dear mirage that would fade away,
So I wrote as tho the house were real.
The book went forth and made appeal
To some far person in some far land,
I know, for a letter came to hand . . .

"Dear Friend," it said "I don't know you,
But I am a dreamer and vagabond, too,
And the house you built of fragile stuff
Is the same as mine. If we dream enough,
If we strive and work, I truly feel
That we can make our houses *real*.
And if mine comes true and I build some day
A house of wood or stone or clay
In a summer land by a drowsy sea,
I hope you will come and visit me
For the door will open to rooms beyond
For poet and artist and vagabond,
A cozy chair, and the table set,
A book and a drink and a cigarette
A shaded light with an orange glow—
All of the things we love and know,
It may be never, it may be soon,
But I hope that maybe some afternoon
I'll hear a step on the creaking stair . . .
I'll open the door and you'll be there
                    Yours, a vagabond."

Address—
    "A God-forgotten Spot," South Africa.

COLORS OF PARADISE

Oh, it's color . . . color . . . color . . .
Lovely, lavish living color
From the green that's in the mountains
To the blue that's in the sea.

Sudden flame of red hibiscus
burning hotly in the hedges . . .

    bronze and russet, rust and henna
    In the wayside-growing crotons . . .

flaunting pompoms of vermilion,
gay uxoria . . . . . . magenta
in the torn and tattered drapery
of the strident bougainvillea . . .

    sullen red above the mountains
    in a grand barbaric sunset . . .

burning worlds in Kilauea . . .
lava, like a flow of life-blood . . .

    rouge . . . a carmine invitation
    on the lips of gaudy geisha . . .

and the flaming poinciana
is a regal scarlet challenge.
blue . . . the quiet of evening
and the singing blue of morning . . .

    in the ocean, pure lapis . . .
    fluid sapphire in the shallows.

moonstone blue in morning glories.
faded, wistful blue plumbago . . .

in the shadows of the valleys
minor blue . . . the blue of cellos . .

harsh metallic blue of peacocks
on an obi . . . blue medallions.

yellows . . . citron, orange, lemon
in the treasures of the fruit-stall

guinea gold in alamada . . .
shower trees all dripping sun-gold . . .

leis of flower-gold, ilima.
yellow ivory . . . Chinese faces.
a thousand greens on the mountains . . .

a thousand greens in the ocean. . . . . . jade
beneath the lacy crest of Queen's surf at
Waikiki . . . silver green armies of kukui
storming the ramparts of the Pali . . . .
lush, pulpy green marsh plants . . . . . beach
vines trailing serpents of vanished green across
the sand.
    sentimental lavender of water hyacinths
. . . . . intricate purple and mauve in the sym-
bolism of passion flowers . . . . . . purple iris
. . . . maroon and green-bronze avocado . . .
the delicate grotesqueries of orchids.
    the rainbow . . . a bridge of fire-opals
leading the uncertain footsteps of our imagin-
ings from a world of drab realities to the
dream-tinted land of illusion. . .
    the lunar rainbow . . . . . ghost of the
glorious day-arch, down which move the weary
phantom figures of the past trailing faded colors
of old exquisite pains, half-forgotten raptures
and dim ecstasies . . . the colors of paradise.

Sea Butterflies

Gay little fishes with painted scales,
Gossamer fins and chiffon tails,
Spattered with jewel dust, stained with dyes,
Gems of jade and jet for eyes,

Striped with orange and smeared with blue,
Dipped in the rainbow's every hue.

Little ones, yellow as buttercups,
Big ones, ugly as gutter-pups,
Fat ones, bloated and marked like toads
Squatted by submarine forest roads.

Fishes gilded with guinea-gold,
Shaped like mythical beasts of old,
Some are enameled like cloissonne,
Lacquered and penciled with colors gay,

Broidered and traced like a Persian shawl,
Fishes that swim and fishes that crawl,
Splotched and daubed in a cubist scheme,
Some are born of a mad man's dream.

FISHES with whiskers and fishes with horns
Just like the fabulous unicorn's
Colors that burn like a funeral pyre,
Colors as pale as a moonstone's fire,
Ochre and amethyst, ultramarine,
Umber, amber and macaw green,
Fragments of fancy, living a day,
Going their curious deep-sea way.

Gay little fishes with painted scales,
Long may you wave your chiffon tails.

HAPPINESS

I thought I knew the meaning of the word
    But you have made a song of it for me.
A song . . . it's rhythmic cadences I've heard
    In all my heart's hot pulsing. Ecstacy
That soars to bird-notes when your cool sweet
      lips
    Rest on my eyes or press my lips apart,
Melody made by your dear finger-tips
    Brushing the strings of my responsive heart.

DAWN IN THE ISLANDS

Black out of blackness . . . mountains taking
    form . . .
    The sun behind gray clouds . . . a hint of
    rain . . .
    And colors seeping into things again . . .
Shy green, pale blue and yellow, thinly warm.

SKETCH
Morning on the Beach

THE day awakening, drowsily opening its eyes . . . air like soft wine, deceptive in its smooth-tasting strength . . . yellow sand yielding beneath your feet like cool golden grain . . . your skin gloriously responsive to the first warmth of the virile sun and the velvety caress of the salt-tanged breeze . . . for a swift moment you are part of the dawn, the sky and the earth.

The sea froths into patterns of foamy lace and slides back with a soft sighing . . .

Mountains rise in ever higher waves of green . . . dark green of koas and white-green of kukui. . . purple shadowed valleys draw long wavering lines from peaks to sea . . . clouds loll lazily on the mountain tops in shell-pink and ice-blue beauty against the pale sky. . . . fringe-crested palms in uncertain parade along the shore . . . beach vines scrawl confusing pictures with their restless tendrils.

lantana spatters the hill slopes with lavender and orange . . . convolvulus lift shy faces to meet the eager glance of the sun . .

tiny sand-crabs tiptoe mincingly about seeking bits of food among the sea-wrack . . . a strong salt odor comes from dark masses of sea-weed abandoned by the careless tide.

a teetering spindle-legged bird utters a wistful 'pwip' and skitters away down the beach

. . .

hold the moment . . . the day is yours to take as you will.

TRUANT RAINBOW

MANOA Rainbow fled one day
From its valley home and hid away
In a little shop where table and stand
Were heaped with loot. On every hand
Lay vivid objects of beauty rare.
The rainbow found concealment there.

It hid its timid twilight blue
In necklaces of Peking Liu
And tiny vases from Cathay
While melancholy purple lay
In amethysts. Bright orange gleamed
On fretted brass until it seemed
The sun had come into the place.
A Chinese doll with ivory face
Took all the rainbow's burning red
To paint her lips. Behind her head
An old brocade benignly let
The rainbow stain it violet.
In shadowed nook and lofty shelf
The rainbow tried to hide itself
In silk-embroidered luncheon cloth,
On tinselled bird or gaudy moth,
In patterned silk and tassels bright,
In turquoise, jade and chrysolite,
In copper bowls and cloisonne
And batik scarf from Mandalay.
About the room from side to side
The startled arch of color tried
To hide its prismy tints away
But you may see it any day
If for a moment you will stop
And look about the Mandarin Shop
In the Young Hotel on the Second floor.
You'll see the name above the door.

VAGABOND'S HEART

I toss my heart, like a leaf, on the breeze
   To fall by the way or to venture far;
   To drift to the earth or to find a star;
The wind may do as the wind may please.

For I am weary of sending my heart
   On joyless journeys down beaten ways,
   Down careful paths on sunny days,
Down roads that are marked on a
         measured chart.

So I fling my heart, like a leaf, on the breeze
   To go the way that the wind may choose
   With a way to find or a way to lose,
And return to me when the wind may please.

TO POETS AND ARTISTS

I would walk with dreamers
Whose highway in life
Is the path of the sun
Across blue waters
Leading to distant mountains.

TWILIGHT

NOW that the shadows of twilight are stealing into the corners of my room I'll open the covers of my favorite books, then, if I sit very still and watch through the weaving gray magic of my cigarette smoke I may see those well-loved characters stepping quietly forth from the thumbed pages . . . . . .

Kim, sunbrowned and impish, vagabonding in the bazaars of India and finding fine life on the high-road to Simla . . .

Huckleberry Finn, heart-brother of Kim, floating on a raft in the Mississippi . . . . . philosopher, poet and great dreamer . . . .

Salammbo, wandering in drugged mystic ecstasy among the white peacocks on the terraces above Carthage . . .

Salome, with rouged finger tips pressed against her gilded eyelids, brooding on her erotic passion for Jokannan . . .

Sonnica of Saguntum tossing the bright bauble of life into the fires of a great renunciation . . . .

Pale Pelleas and paler Melisande suffering the strange fevers of their love. . . .

Galahad, Eve and earthy Adam . . .
Eben Holden, d'Artagnan and Carmen . . .
Moby Dick and Kamehameha . . . .

Camille and Guinivere . . .
Jurgen and Helen of Troy . . .
Cigarette and Joan the Maid . . .
Judith of Bethulia . . .
Perseus with borrowed wings for his heels. .
The raw Yankee who made folly of King
    Arthur's court . . .
Fagin the Jew and Pere Goriot . . .
Dorian Gray with his strange perverse life . .
Dracula . . .
John Silence, doctor of souls . . .
Sheba . . .

One by one they whisper their curious stories until I turn on the lights of evening, arch-enemy of dreams. Even then they are not really gone. If I listen I can hear the rustle of their garments, the echoes of their laughters and the faint murmur of their voices in the corner by the book-shelves.

TO DON MAY . . .
A friend who climbed mountains with me.

WE knew the desolation of great heights
   And the contentment of deep valleys;
We saw the moon leap silver from the mountain peaks
   And watched the red sun die in a welter of mists on the horizon;
We knew the white swift decline of vast snow fields
   And the small beauty of forest flowers;
Our dreams rose with the smoke of our camp fires in the wilderness
   And our friendship glowed with the embers of fir-fires;
We shared hunger, thirst and the great struggle toward the mountain top
   As we shared the peace, good food and pleasant rest of our night camps;
All these things . . . the dizziness of sudden precipices, the turmoil of enveloping clouds, straining muscles, weariness, exhalation, the soothing fragrance of pine trees, the chatter of mountain streams, and the roar of furious rapids entered into the pattern of our friendship and made it fine.
These things we knew together . . .
And these things we will remember.

Walking in beauty as we are . . . sun-gold,
    moon-silver ever in your eyes,
      Treading on flowers. . . breathing per-
        fumed air,
We do forget what loveliness is ours . . . .
    what treasure lies
      Quick to our hands until, all unaware
We come to a sudden corner. . . face the
    sea and clouds, a stretch of sky
      Burning with color, drenched with glory. So,
As one, walking asleep with open eyes, wakens
    to a cry,
      We waken to a beauty which we saw and
        did not know.

YESTERDAY'S MEN

BACK in the days that are dimmed by
      distance,
Back in the days that are told in legend,
These men sailed from a far off island
Sailed in boats that were hewed in the jungle
            They knew hunger
            They knew danger
Storms at sea and the fear of monsters.
            Brought their women
            Brought their children,
Brought the trees and the plants they cherished.

Landed here on an unknown island
Builded houses, planted breadfruit,
            Builded fishponds,
            Builded altars,
Made some new gods, kept some old ones.

Named the islands, named the mountains,
Wove their curious tales about them,
Lived in awe of the great volcano,
Sacrificed to the goddess Pele
            a-a-auwe. . .
            the voice of wailing
            a-a-auwe
            the voice of mourning.

Days of feasting, days of labor,
Days of waging wars and battles,
Days of hunger, days of plenty,
      a-a-auwe
      the poi and mullet
      a-a-auwe
      pig in the imu
Prophets rose and the great kahunas,
Chiefs who were known in war and hunting,
Found the foods that were in the ocean,
Found the herbs that were in the mountains,
      ti for awa,
      ti for houses,
Wove the mats of lauhala,
Wove the nets of bark and fibre.

Heroes lived and established history,
Romance grew in the songs of poets
Beat the drums to rhythmic madness,
Hollow logs with heads of shark-skin,
      bom . . bom. . bom.
      the beat of the war drum
      bom . . bom. . bom. .
      the hula pahu
small pu niu . . seeds in a gourd shell

      . . . .

. . . .

Gone the old gods, gone the fierce ones,
Only shadows in the sunset,
Only voices in the trade winds
        a-a-auwe
        the voice of Maui
        a-a-auwe
        the voice of Lono
Gone are the capes and the feather helmets,
Gone are the songs or half-forgotten,
        Now there are new gods,
        New strange customs,
Seven bloods that are intermingled.

        What is the future,
        What new glories,
What for the sons of chiefs and warriors?
        Yours to determine,
        Yours to vision,
Yours to carry the old tradition,
Hew new boats to sail new oceans
        Make new heroes.
        Young Hawaiians,
Guide your course by the stars of future,
Weave your sails with strands of courage,
Bom-bom-bom—in the sound of thunder
Hear the voice of your father's fathers
        "Go you forward
        Face the future."
Those are the words in the voice of thunder.

A KAMAʻAINA SPEAKS . . . .

Ah, you'll never know Hawaii 'til you've kissed
    an Island girl
      And she's hung a ginger lei around your
        neck;
'Til you've danced the hula-hula on a beach of
    sand and pearl
      And have eaten raw opihis by the peck;

'Til you've hung your every garment on a big
    kamani tree
      And have felt the foaming surf about your
        knees;
'Til you've plunged into the breakers with a
    cry of pagan glee
      In a bathing suit of moonlight and a breeze;

'Til you've seen the lunar rainbow's phantom
    arch across the blue
      And have watched the Southern Cross dip
      in the sea;
'Til the singing boys have stabbed your heart
    with music–thru and thru
      'Til you've raced the silver surf at Waikiki;

'Til you've slid down Ginger Jack–and every
    youngster knows the place
      'Til you've gorged on pig until you couldn't
      think;
'Til you've seen the path of fury strewn with
    white-hot lava lace
      Where red Pele walks at Kilauea's brink.

'Til you've heard the old folks yarning of the
    days before today
    At a luau over bowls of fish and poi;
'Til you've gone aboard a steamer with intent
    to stay away
    And have learned the meaning of
    "Aloha Oe."

'Til you've been so blinking homesick for these
    Islands of the Sun
    That you simply couldn't stand it any more
And you've chucked your things together—
    bought a ticket on the run
    And have headed for Hawaii's lovely shore;

'Til you've felt your tonsils quiver when the
    tears begin to start
    As old Diamond Head looms black against
    the sky;
NO, you're just a malihini 'til you've felt
    down in your heart
    That your home—I mean your home is in
    Hawaii.

WAIKIKI

(steel guitar)

Sea asleep . . . except for restless sighing;
    Drowsy moon . . . above the trade-clouds
      showing;
    Lazy palms . . . their ragged banners throwing
Shadow lace upon the figures lying

(ukulele)

    Sprawling in the moonlight,
      Strumming ukulele,
      Fellow humming gaily
    Song about a June night.

(guitar)

Pretty girl . . . her eyes with dreaming soften;
    Lucky chap . . his arms are close about her;
    Whispered words . . . he can not live with-
      out her;
Drowsy moon . . . has watched the scene so
    often.

HOMESICK FOR THE ISLANDS
In New York

TODAY I passed a tiny florist shop
   With hurried step . . . a fragrance made
   me stop
And look with sudden, wistful, homesick stare.
A bowl of pale gardenias beckoned there
Behind the glass. So white! So deeply green
The leaves! Auwe, how often have I seen
The hedges starred with those soft velvet
   flowers.
How often has their fragrance perfumed hours
Of high romance in Flapper's Acre--Waikiki--
Auwe! I'm homesick as can be.

ALOHA OE

One lei I'll wear . . . it will not fade
   One lei I need not put away
     When I go out to sea some day . .
A lei that Island memories made.

A gorgeous lei . . . a golden lei
   Aloha threaded on a string
     Of happiness. A lei to bring
Me back; when I am far away.

Books by the
PETROGLYPH PRESS